CONTENTS

The Anxious Thumb: unfiltred living in a filtred world	1
Dr. Samantha Mitchell	2
CONTENUTI	4
Chapter 1:	5
Chapter 2:	10
Chapter 3:	16
Chapter 4:	22
Chapter 5:	28
Chapter 6:	34
Chapter 7:	40
About	46
Dr. Samantha Mitchell	47

THE ANXIOUS THUMB: UNFILTRED LIVING IN A FILTRED WORLD

DR. SAMANTHA MITCHELL

Copyright © 2024 By Dr. Samantha Mitchell
Leonardo Publishing
All Right Reserved

CONTENUTI

	Ringraziamenti	i
1	Nome capitolo	1
2	Nome capitolo	N. pag.
3	Nome capitolo	N. pag.
4	Nome capitolo	N. pag.
5	Nome capitolo	N. pag.
6	Nome capitolo	N. pag.
7	Nome capitolo	N. pag.
8	Nome capitolo	N. pag.
9	Nome capitolo	N. pag.
10	Nome capitolo	N. pag.

CHAPTER 1:

Welcome to the Anxiety Age

Imagine this: It's the year 2024. You wake up, reach for your phone, and before you even brush your teeth, you're already scrolling through a dozen apps. Instagram, TikTok, whatever news feed caught your attention last night. Your brain's barely woken up, but your anxiety? It's already in fifth gear.

Welcome to the *Anxiety Age*.

If you're feeling overwhelmed just by reading this, you're not alone. Anxiety isn't just that occasional knot in your stomach anymore—it's become the soundtrack of our lives. Especially for those born after 1995, the so-called Gen Z, anxiety has become as common as Wi-Fi signals.

Why the Fuss About Gen Z?

Gen Z is unique. They're the first generation to hit puberty with a portal to an alternate universe—a universe we call *the internet*. In the past, kids were worried about acne or who to sit next to at lunch. Now? They're worried about how many likes their latest post gets, or whether an online troll is going to turn their life upside down with one viral tweet.

In just a few years, Gen Z has transitioned from playgrounds to pixels, from real-world interactions to endless scrolling. Childhoods that used to be full of scraped knees and playground drama have been replaced with screen time, algorithm-driven rabbit holes, and an alarming increase in anxiety.

The statistics back this up: Studies in 2024 show that more than 70% of teens report feeling anxious on a daily basis. For many, that anxiety isn't just the typical stress over schoolwork or peer pressure—it's a deep, constant sense of dread that's difficult to shake.

From Helicopter Parents to Helicopter Minds

Back in the day, we worried about parents being too overprotective—"helicopter parents," hovering over their kids. Well, now it's the kids' minds that are doing the hovering. Gen Z isn't just worrying about the usual things teens worry about—dating, grades, future careers. They're worrying about everything, all the time.

How did we get here?

Simple. We've created a culture of hyperconnectivity. While parents were busy wrapping their kids in bubble wrap, making sure they never scraped a knee or felt a moment of discomfort in the real world, they left them unsupervised in the digital world. What happened? They became the guinea pigs of an experiment called social media, and it hasn't been pretty.

The Digital Gold Rush: How We Got Hooked

Back in the early 2000s, tech companies were like modern-day Prometheans, bringing us the gift of technology. Everything felt like it was going to make life better—more connected, more efficient, more *fun*. What could possibly go wrong?

Fast forward to 2024, and we have a generation that's practically glued to their screens. The dopamine hit of a *"like"* or a new follower feels great—until it doesn't. And when it doesn't? Welcome to anxiety. Studies show that the more time teens spend online, the worse they feel. It's not just about FOMO (fear of missing out); it's about real, measurable mental health declines. Depression rates have skyrocketed, especially among girls, who tend to be more affected by the constant comparison game that social media creates.

Let's face it: We've all been there. That weird sense of unease when you see someone else's perfect life plastered all over Instagram. You know it's probably staged, but your brain doesn't care. You scroll, you compare, you feel bad—and then you scroll some more.

Why Anxiety Loves the Internet

Why is anxiety thriving in the digital age? For one, our brains aren't built to process the kind of constant, high-speed information flow we get online. We evolved to deal with real-world threats—saber-tooth tigers, not Instagram influencers. When your brain sees something stressful online, it triggers the same *"fight or flight"* response that it would if you were being chased by a wild animal. Only, there's no wild animal—it's just a post on Facebook.

This constant activation of the brain's stress response wears us down. It's why so many teens today report feeling *"wired but tired."* They're hyperconnected, but deeply disconnected from the things that really matter, like real-life friendships, outdoor play, and those important face-to-face interactions that help us navigate the world.

The Real Cost of Living Online

It's not just anxiety and depression that are on the rise. The impact of social media on Gen Z's attention span, sleep, and overall mental health is staggering. In fact, a study published in 2024 found that teens are sleeping an average of two hours less per night than they were just a decade ago. Why? Because they're spending their nights scrolling through TikTok instead of getting the rest their brains desperately need.

And let's not even get started on attention spans. The age of information overload has left many teens—and adults—with the attention span of a goldfish. Studies show that our brains are literally being rewired by the constant influx of notifications, memes, and content.

Is There Hope?

But don't despair. It's not all doom and gloom. The good news is that awareness is growing, and steps are being taken to address the problem. Schools, parents, and even governments are starting to realize that something needs to change. From limiting screen time to creating "device-free" zones, there are ways to curb the effects of the digital world.

But most importantly, we need to start having real conversations—conversations about mental health, about how we use technology, and about how we can reclaim our lives from the constant churn of anxiety.

In the next chapters, we'll dive deeper into the science of what's really going on in our brains and explore how we can find balance in an increasingly unbalanced world.

So buckle up. The Age of Anxiety is here, but it doesn't have to be the end of the story.

CHAPTER 2:

The Scroll Trap: How Social Media Hijacked Our Lives

Let's face it, we've all been there. You open your phone to check the weather or reply to a message, and suddenly it's two hours later, and you're knee-deep in conspiracy theories about lizard people ruling the world. Welcome to the scroll trap—a digital black hole from which no one escapes unscathed.

Social media was supposed to connect us, right? Keep us in touch with faraway friends and give us a platform to express ourselves. But what was once a fun way to kill time has turned into a full-blown addiction. In 2024, the average person spends over **6 hours a day** on social media, and that's not counting time spent aimlessly scrolling through TikTok at 2 a.m., trying to soothe existential dread with cat videos.

The Birth of the Infinite Scroll

If you thought social media addiction was just a byproduct of our modern lifestyle, think again. It was *engineered* to be that way. Back in the early 2010s, a sinister invention crept into our lives: the infinite scroll. That little feature, which lets you scroll endlessly without hitting a bottom, has rewired our brains to keep consuming content like it's potato chips at a party. And much like potato chips, once you start, you can't stop.

CHAPTER 2:

Companies like Facebook, Instagram, and Twitter (now X, but come on, it's still Twitter) invested billions into figuring out how to keep you scrolling for as long as possible. They hire behavioral psychologists to optimize the exact timing of notifications, the placement of "like" buttons, and the order of posts. Their goal? Keep you hooked. And boy, has it worked.

By 2024, the addiction has reached new heights. We're no longer just talking about endless cat memes and *"influencers"* selling you teeth-whitening kits. No, now we have AI-powered content generators that know exactly what you want to see before you even know you want to see it. It's like mind control, but with dance challenges and hashtag activism.

The Rise of the 10-Second Dopamine Hit

Social media platforms aren't just fun—they're scientifically designed to hijack your brain's dopamine circuits. And if you don't know what dopamine is, it's the little chemical in your brain responsible for pleasure. Every time you get a like, a retweet, or a comment on your post, your brain releases a little burst of dopamine. It feels good—really good. So, naturally, you want more.

Fast forward to 2024, and we've reached the pinnacle of dopamine-driven entertainment: the 10-second video. TikTok, Instagram Reels, and YouTube Shorts are perfect examples of this. These short, fast-paced videos are designed to deliver maximum pleasure in minimal time. It's like a slot machine, but instead of cash, you're gambling for attention.

And the scariest part? It's working. Studies published in 2024 show that teens spend an average of 4 hours per day on short-form video apps. These apps are so addictive because they provide quick, unpredictable rewards—

exactly like a casino. You never know when you're going to find that next viral video that will give you the dopamine hit you've been craving.

The AI Content Overlords

In 2024, we've entered a new era of social media where AI is calling the shots. Platforms like TikTok and Instagram don't just serve you what your friends are posting—they serve you content generated by advanced algorithms that know you better than you know yourself.

You ever wonder why your *"For You"* page feels eerily accurate? That's because artificial intelligence is constantly learning from your behaviors, tracking what you watch, how long you watch it, and whether you hit "like" or scroll past it. The AI doesn't care if you're happy, sad, or spiraling into a pit of anxiety—it just wants to keep you scrolling. It's like a personal shopper, but for your attention span, and the only currency is your mental health.

And let's not forget the role AI plays in *creating* content. In 2024, AI-generated influencers, entire fictional worlds, and even virtual pets are becoming mainstream. These digital beings are designed to look perfect, act perfect, and make you feel inferior in the process. But hey, at least they're consistent, right?

Kids, Screens, and the New Attention Deficit Disorder

Now, let's talk about the real victims of the scroll trap: Gen Z and the emerging Generation Alpha. These kids have grown up in a world where iPads were the new pacifiers, and YouTube was their nanny. And the results? Not great.

Studies in 2024 show that the average attention span of teens has dropped from **12 seconds in 2000 to just 8 seconds** today. For context, that's **one second shorter than**

a goldfish. This might explain why multitasking is now just a fancy word for "*doing a lot of things poorly.*"

But it's not just attention spans that are suffering. **Sleep deprivation** is at an all-time high, thanks to the fact that teens are spending more time on their phones in bed than actually sleeping. A study from this year found that **60% of teens** sleep with their phones within arm's reach, and more than **half check social media within 10 minutes of waking up**. Talk about starting the day with a side of anxiety.

The FOMO Epidemic

One of the biggest reasons people can't put down their phones is FOMO—fear of missing out. It's not just a catchy acronym; it's a real psychological phenomenon that drives social media addiction. Platforms are designed to make you feel like everyone is living a better life than you, and if you don't check your feed every five minutes, you'll miss out on something important (spoiler alert: you won't).

In 2024, FOMO has evolved into something even darker. Now, it's not just about missing out on what your friends are doing—it's about missing out on the *trending conversation*, the viral meme, or the political debate that everyone is talking about. And if you're not in the loop? Well, good luck trying to catch up.

Social Media: The New Big Tobacco?

Remember when smoking was cool, and then we realized it was literally killing people? Well, social media is kind of like that. It started as something harmless—just a fun way to connect with friends. But now, it's becoming clear that the long-term effects are seriously damaging.

Recent studies in 2024 have likened social media addiction to smoking in the 1950s. At first, no one thought much of it. But now, we're seeing the long-term consequences, particularly on mental health. Depression, anxiety, loneliness, and body image issues are all on the rise, and social media is one of the main culprits.

The difference? Big Tobacco had to hide its research on how harmful cigarettes were. Social media platforms don't need to hide anything—they've just made us too addicted to care.

Can We Break Free?

Here's the million-dollar question: Can we escape the scroll trap? The short answer is yes—but not without effort. Some researchers suggest going on a "**digital detox**", limiting your screen time, or setting boundaries for when and where you use your phone.

But let's be real: It's not easy to quit cold turkey when the whole world is online 24/7. What we need isn't just individual willpower—we need systemic change. Governments and tech companies need to step up and create regulations that protect our mental health. We need education on digital literacy and the importance of real-world connections.

And most importantly, we need to remember that there's a whole world out there beyond our screens. A world where conversations happen face-to-face, where experiences aren't filtered through a lens, and where the only thing you're scrolling through is the pages of a good book.

So the next time you find yourself caught in the scroll trap, take a deep breath, put down your phone, and look up. The real world is waiting for you—and trust me, it's way more interesting than any TikTok dance challenge.

In the next chapter, we'll explore how this digital addiction is affecting our youngest generation and what we can do to protect them. Because if we don't act now, we might just scroll our way into a future none of us want to live in.

CHAPTER 3:

The Disappearing Childhood: From Playgrounds to Phones

Close your eyes for a second and try to remember your childhood. If you were born before 2000, there's a good chance you're picturing long afternoons spent outside, climbing trees, playing tag, or maybe even riding bikes until the streetlights came on. Now, fast-forward to 2024, and what do kids do today? They swipe, they tap, they scroll.

It's not that kids don't play anymore. They do—it's just that their *"playgrounds"* have moved from the neighborhood park to the glowing screens of their devices. Childhood, once filled with scraped knees and muddy sneakers, has been replaced by hours of screen time, and it's reshaping not just how kids spend their time, but how they grow up.

The Death of Free Play

It wasn't that long ago when *"go outside and play"* was the default activity for kids. It didn't require scheduling, parental supervision, or GPS tracking. You just opened the door and ran until your lungs ached and your imagination had taken you to a dozen different worlds.

But today, that's not the reality. Kids aren't running around unsupervised. They're not making up rules for games or building forts out of fallen branches. Instead, they're locked inside, tapping through virtual worlds created by game developers. The concept of *"free play"* has been replaced by structured, screen-mediated activities.

Don't believe it? Here's a sobering statistic: In 2024, the average 10-year-old spends **seven hours a day** in front of a screen. That's more time than they spend sleeping. And what about time outdoors? Less than **one hour** a day. It's no wonder today's kids are more familiar with Minecraft than they are with actual dirt.

The Decline of Social Skills

The biggest casualty of the disappearing childhood isn't just the loss of physical play—it's the loss of social skills. Remember the playground politics of childhood? Negotiating turns on the swing, deciding who would be *"it"* in tag, or working out disputes over whose imaginary rules were the right ones? Those interactions were vital training grounds for real life.

But as kids have retreated into their screens, those social interactions have become fewer and farther between. Now, their *"conversations"* are happening through emojis, TikTok duets, and Instagram comments. Sure, they're communicating—but are they really *connecting*?

A 2024 study found that **75% of kids** aged 8 to 12 prefer texting over face-to-face communication. That means most kids would rather send a message than talk to someone in person, and this shift is having consequences. Social anxiety among teens is at an all-time high, and experts believe the decline in real-life interactions is a major reason why.

Helicopter Parents and Screen-Time Babysitters

So, how did we get here? Part of the answer lies with the rise of *helicopter parenting*. Back in the 1980s and 90s, parents started becoming more and more protective, worried about "*stranger danger*" and the perils of an unmonitored childhood. Playgrounds were deemed too risky, and parents hovered over their kids like drones on a surveillance mission.

As a result, kids started staying indoors more, and screens became the perfect digital babysitter. Parents, looking for a way to keep their kids entertained and safe, handed over iPads and smartphones. What could go wrong? At least they're not getting hurt, right?

Well, not exactly. What started as a way to keep kids occupied quickly spiraled into full-blown dependency. And now, parents are left with children who are more comfortable in the digital world than in the real one. A recent study revealed that **60% of parents** admit they use screens to "calm" their kids down or to keep them busy during meals. It's no longer about keeping them entertained—it's about keeping them pacified.

The Lost Art of Play

What's even more tragic is that we've forgotten the importance of *play*. Real play. The kind that doesn't involve level-ups, virtual rewards, or follower counts. Unstructured play is crucial for developing creativity, problem-solving skills, and emotional resilience. When kids run around, make mistakes, and figure out how to work together, they're learning valuable life lessons—ones that can't be taught through a screen.

In 2024, children spend most of their free time glued to a device. Playgrounds sit empty, and even when kids are outside, they're often absorbed in their phones. The spontaneous joy of running, falling, laughing, and getting back up is being lost to the carefully curated, screen-mediated *"experiences"* designed by tech companies.

Studies show that children who engage in less physical play are more likely to experience ***anxiety***, ***depression***, and ***difficulty concentrating***. Yet, the trend continues—because physical play can be messy, unpredictable, and risky. Digital play? It's safe, controlled, and convenient.

Government and Educational Interventions: Too Little, Too Late?

Fortunately, the issue hasn't gone unnoticed. As the data on screen time and its negative effects continue to pile up, governments and educators around the world are starting to take action. In 2024, several countries have introduced **legislation** aimed at limiting screen time for children under 12. In France, for instance, new laws mandate that schools create *"tech-free"* zones and restrict the use of smartphones during school hours.

In Japan, a country where screen addiction among children has reached critical levels, new *after-school programs* focused on outdoor play have been introduced in urban areas, with the aim of getting kids off their devices and back into nature. These programs are backed by research showing that even *two hours a week* of unstructured outdoor play can significantly reduce stress levels and improve cognitive function in children.

In the United States, many schools have adopted similar

policies, banning phones during class time and introducing mindfulness and meditation programs to counteract the effects of digital overload. But despite these efforts, the shift is slow. For every initiative aimed at getting kids off screens, there are a hundred new apps designed to keep them on.

A New Model for Childhood

So, what can we do to reclaim childhood? Is it possible to bring back the free-spirited, playful days of yore in a world dominated by technology? The answer might lie in finding a balance—one that encourages both screen time and real-world time, while acknowledging the importance of letting kids just *be kids.*

Some schools and communities are experimenting with **outdoor education programs,** where kids spend half their day learning outside, regardless of the weather. These programs are not only teaching academic subjects, but also building resilience, curiosity, and a connection to nature. And the results are promising. In Sweden, where outdoor play is a core part of the education system, children report lower levels of anxiety and higher levels of happiness than in most other developed nations.

In New Zealand, some schools are experimenting with "*technology-free*" weeks, where students leave their devices at home and focus on hands-on learning. Early results show that kids are more engaged, less distracted, and, surprisingly, *happier* when they're not constantly checking their phones.

CHAPTER 3:

A Future Where Play Matters Again

We may not be able to completely turn back the clock, but we can start to reimagine childhood in a way that includes both the digital and the physical worlds. It's not about eliminating technology—it's about finding a balance that allows children to grow up with the same sense of wonder, curiosity, and adventure that we once had.

Playgrounds may be disappearing, but that doesn't mean childhood has to. It's up to us to create spaces, both literal and figurative, where kids can be kids again—where they can run, explore, fall, and get back up. Where the biggest challenge isn't getting to the next level in a video game, but climbing to the top of the jungle gym.
The future of childhood depends on it.

In the next chapter, we'll explore how parenting styles have evolved (or devolved) in the digital age, and what we can do to raise resilient, balanced kids in a world that seems determined to keep them glued to screens.

CHAPTER 4:

How We Got Here: Fear, Overprotection, and Helicopter Parenting

Remember when parents would say things like, "*Go outside and don't come back until dinner,*" and that was totally normal? Well, those days are long gone. Today's parents are more likely to say, "*Don't forget your sunscreen, your helmet, and your GPS tracker.*" And if you think I'm exaggerating, I've got news for you—I'm not.

Over the last few decades, we've seen the rise of a new breed of parenting: *helicopter parenting.* You know the type. Parents who hover so closely over their children, you'd think they were getting paid to be full-time bodyguards. The result? A generation of kids who are overprotected, underprepared, and, well, anxious.

How did we get here? Buckle up—it's a wild ride of fear, anxiety, and a few too many "*Stranger Danger*" PSAs.

The Age of Fear

It all started in the late 20th century, when a handful of high-profile child abductions and media-fueled panic made parents terrified to let their kids out of their sight. Suddenly, the world felt like a much scarier place, even though statistically speaking, it wasn't. In fact, crime rates have been steadily dropping since the 1990s, but you wouldn't know it from the way parents act.

By the early 2000s, parents had become obsessed with safety. It wasn't enough to make sure your child wore a seatbelt—you had to wrap them in bubble wrap and follow them everywhere to ensure nothing bad ever happened. This overprotective mindset gave birth to the phenomenon we now know as helicopter parenting.

Fast forward to 2024, and we're still living in the shadow of that fear. Only now, we have a new villain: technology. Parents today aren't just worried about kidnappers—they're worried about *the internet*. They're terrified of the endless dangers lurking online: cyberbullying, inappropriate content, and of course, the ever-present risk of their child accidentally ordering $500 worth of Pokémon cards from Amazon.

Helicopter Parenting: A Love Story Gone Wrong

Let's be clear: helicopter parenting comes from a place of love. Parents just want to keep their kids safe. But somewhere along the way, that well-intentioned love turned into an obsession with controlling every aspect of their child's life. From playdates to homework to what they're eating for lunch, no detail is too small to micromanage.

And the result? A generation of kids who are anxious, risk-averse, and dependent. Studies in 2024 show that children raised by helicopter parents are more likely to experience ***anxiety disorders*** and ***low self-esteem*** than their peers. Why? Because they've never been given the chance to fail. When you grow up with someone constantly hovering over you, making sure you never fall, you never learn how to pick yourself back up.

Think about it: if you've never scraped your knee, how are you supposed to know that you can survive it?

The Pandemic: Helicopter Parenting on Steroids

Then, just when you thought things couldn't get more intense, along came the COVID-19 pandemic—a global crisis tailor-made for overprotective parents. Suddenly, the world really *was* dangerous, and keeping your child safe became a full-time job. Parents didn't just hover—they quarantined, sanitized, and locked down. And honestly? Who can blame them?

But here's the thing: while the pandemic may have justified a certain level of overprotection, it also supercharged the helicopter mindset. Studies in 2024 show that parental anxiety reached all-time highs during the pandemic, and it hasn't fully subsided. Parents who were already inclined to overprotect became even more controlling, and kids who were already struggling with anxiety found themselves trapped in a world where fear was the default setting.

The long-term effects of this pandemic-era parenting style are still being studied, but early results are concerning. Kids who grew up in the shadow of COVID-19 are showing higher rates of **social anxiety**, **agoraphobia**, and **dependence on parental approval** than previous generations. It's not just that they're afraid of getting sick—they're afraid of *everything*.

The Cost of Never Letting Go

Here's the harsh truth: kids need to be given the space to make mistakes. They need to fall down, screw up, and learn from it. But when parents step in to fix every problem, kids never get the chance to develop the resilience they need to navigate life's challenges.

By 2024, we have a whole generation that's struggling to handle the basic challenges of adulthood. From managing their own schedules to dealing with disappointment, many young adults are finding themselves woefully unprepared for life outside their parents' safety net.

And it's not just the kids who suffer—*parents* are feeling the strain, too. Studies show that helicopter parents experience higher levels of **stress** and **burnout** than their more hands-off counterparts. After all, managing someone else's life is exhausting.

In fact, a 2024 survey revealed that **65% of parents** feel overwhelmed by the demands of modern parenting, and many admit that they're struggling to let go as their children grow older. It's a vicious cycle: the more parents hover, the more dependent kids become, and the more dependent kids become, the more parents feel the need to hover.

Are We Really Protecting Them?

The irony of helicopter parenting is that, in trying to protect their children, parents may actually be doing more harm than good. By shielding kids from every possible risk, we're not teaching them how to handle risk—we're teaching them to avoid it altogether.

Take this example: A child who's never been allowed to cross the street on their own grows up afraid of cars. They've been told that the street is dangerous, so they never learn how to navigate it safely. Now, imagine that same child as an adult. They still don't know how to cross the street—only now, there's no one there to hold their hand.

In 2024, mental health experts are sounding the alarm. They warn that our culture of overprotection is creating a generation that's ill-equipped to handle life's challenges. Kids aren't learning the critical skills they need—like problem-solving, emotional regulation, and resilience—

because they're never put in situations where they have to use them.

Finding a Middle Ground

So, how do we break the cycle of helicopter parenting without throwing caution to the wind? The key, experts say, is finding a balance between protection and independence. Kids need to know that their parents are there for them, but they also need the freedom to take risks, make mistakes, and learn from them.

In 2024, many schools and communities are starting to adopt a new approach to parenting and education called "*scaffolded independence*". This approach encourages parents to provide support when necessary, but also to step back and let their kids take charge of their own lives when appropriate. It's about teaching kids *how* to solve problems, rather than solving the problems for them.

Some schools have even started incorporating "*resilience training*" into their curriculums, teaching kids how to manage stress, navigate challenges, and build emotional intelligence. These programs are designed to counteract the effects of overprotection by giving kids the tools they need to thrive in the real world.

The Future of Parenting

As we look to the future, one thing is clear: we need to rethink how we approach parenting. It's time to let go of the helicopter, step back from the control panel, and trust that our kids are capable of handling more than we give them credit for.

Sure, the world can be scary. But shielding our children from every possible danger isn't the answer. Instead, we need to equip them with the skills, confidence, and resilience to face that world head-on.

So, to all the parents out there: take a deep breath, loosen your grip, and give your kids the space they need to grow. They'll thank you for it—eventually.

In the next chapter, we'll explore the unique challenges faced by girls in the digital age, and why anxiety seems to hit them particularly hard. It's time to unpack the gender gap in mental health and what we can do about it.

CHAPTER 5:

The Gender Gap: Why Anxiety Hits Girls Harder

Let's get one thing straight: anxiety doesn't discriminate. It's an equal opportunity affliction that strikes everyone, regardless of gender, age, or background. But here's the kicker: it seems to hit girls a lot harder. And no, it's not because they're more *"emotional"* or *"fragile"*—it's because the world we've created for them is a pressure cooker of impossible standards, social comparison, and digital noise.

In 2024, the data is crystal clear: girls experience significantly higher levels of anxiety and depression than boys. They're also more likely to suffer from body image issues, social stress, and a host of other mental health challenges. But why? What is it about being a girl today that makes anxiety feel like a permanent roommate?

The Perfect Storm of Social Pressure

Let's start with the obvious: girls are under an immense amount of social pressure. From a young age, they're bombarded with messages about how they should look, act, and even think. By the time they hit puberty, they're walking a tightrope of expectations—be smart, but not too smart; be confident, but not too confident; be pretty, but not too pretty. It's exhausting just thinking about it.

Now, throw in social media, and that pressure goes from a

simmer to a full boil.

In 2024, girls spend an average of four hours a day on social media platforms like Instagram and TikTok. These platforms aren't just fun distractions—they're curated, polished versions of reality that make it impossible not to compare yourself to others. For girls, the pressure to look perfect, be liked, and fit into societal standards is magnified tenfold by the constant stream of filtered images and highlight reels.

A 2024 study found that 70% of teenage girls feel worse about their bodies after spending time on social media. And it's not hard to see why. Every day, they're scrolling through photos of influencers and celebrities who look flawless (thanks to a mix of professional lighting, Photoshop, and good genes), and it's hard not to feel like they're falling short in comparison.

TikTok and the Rise of the *"Ideal"* Girl

TikTok, in particular, has become a battleground for self-esteem. The app's algorithm is designed to show users exactly what they want to see—and for teenage girls, that often means an endless loop of beauty tutorials, fashion trends, and fitness routines. While some of this content can be empowering, much of it reinforces narrow, unattainable beauty standards.

In 2024, we're seeing the effects of this play out in real time. Girls are more likely than boys to suffer from body dysmorphia, a mental health condition where they obsess over perceived flaws in their appearance. And while movements like body positivity and body neutrality have gained traction in recent years, the pressure to conform to an idealized image remains strong—especially on platforms like TikTok, where going viral often depends on how you look.

It's not just about body image, though. TikTok has also created a new kind of social pressure: the pressure to perform. On TikTok, everything is a performance, from your morning skincare routine to your dance moves. For girls, this can create a sense of constant surveillance, where they feel like they're always being watched, judged, and evaluated. It's no wonder that anxiety is through the roof.

The Silent Epidemic of Social Anxiety

Speaking of anxiety, let's talk about social anxiety—because girls are feeling it more than ever. While boys tend to express their stress through external behaviors (like aggression or acting out), girls are more likely to internalize their anxiety, leading to issues like social withdrawal, overthinking, and a constant fear of judgment.

In 2024, more than 50% of teenage girls report experiencing social anxiety, compared to just 30% of boys. This isn't just about being shy—it's about feeling a deep, overwhelming sense of dread in social situations. And with the rise of social media, the lines between online and offline interactions have blurred, making it even harder for girls to escape the pressure to present a "perfect" version of themselves.

The pandemic didn't help, either. Many girls spent crucial developmental years in isolation, communicating primarily through screens. Now, as they re-enter the world of in-person interactions, they're finding it harder than ever to navigate social situations without feeling overwhelmed. Studies show that the rates of social anxiety among girls skyrocketed during the COVID-19 pandemic and have remained high ever since.

The Gendered Impact of Body Image

Let's circle back to body image for a minute, because this is where the gender gap in anxiety really starts to show. While boys also face pressure to look a certain way (thanks, muscle-bound superheroes), the standards for girls are far more pervasive and unattainable.

In 2024, 65% of girls between the ages of 12 and 18 report feeling dissatisfied with their bodies. That's compared to 35% of boys. What's worse, girls as young as 10 are already worrying about their weight, shape, and appearance—long before they've even finished growing.

Part of the problem is that society still places an enormous amount of value on a woman's appearance. While boys are often praised for their achievements, girls are more likely to be judged based on how they look. And with the rise of social media, that judgment has become more public and more relentless.

Movements like body positivity have made some headway in changing the conversation around beauty standards, encouraging girls to embrace their bodies as they are. But in 2024, the reality is that the pressures haven't gone away—they've just become more insidious. Girls are now expected not only to look perfect but to love the way they look, no matter what. It's a double-edged sword: if you don't fit the beauty ideal, you're not good enough—and if you don't love your imperfections, you're still falling short.

Why Girls Are More Vulnerable to Anxiety

So, why do girls experience anxiety more intensely than boys? It's not just because of social media and body image—it's also biological. Research shows that hormonal changes during puberty make girls more susceptible to anxiety. The fluctuations in estrogen and progesterone that occur during adolescence can affect mood regulation and increase sensitivity to stress.

But it's not all biology. Socialization plays a big role, too. From a young age, girls are taught to be more attuned to their emotions and the emotions of others. While this emotional intelligence can be a strength, it also means that girls are more likely to take on the weight of other people's expectations and judgments. They're taught to be people-pleasers, to avoid conflict, and to put others' needs before their own—and that can lead to a lot of internalized stress and anxiety.

By the time they reach adolescence, many girls are juggling the pressure to succeed academically, socially, and physically—all while maintaining an image of effortless perfection. It's no wonder they're feeling overwhelmed.

The Fight for Mental Health Support

Thankfully, the mental health conversation is changing. In 2024, there's more awareness than ever about the challenges girls face, and schools and communities are starting to take action. Programs that promote mindfulness, self-compassion, and resilience are becoming more common, giving girls the tools they need to manage their anxiety and build confidence.

There's also a growing movement to hold social media platforms accountable for the impact they have on mental health. In some countries, new regulations are being introduced that require platforms like TikTok and Instagram to provide users with mental health resources and to reduce the amount of harmful content related to body image and self-esteem.

But while these efforts are a step in the right direction, there's still a long way to go. Girls today are growing up in a world that's more connected, more competitive, and more scrutinized than ever before. And until we start changing the way we talk about beauty, success, and self-worth, anxiety will continue to hit girls the hardest.

A Way Forward

So, what's the solution? How do we start closing the gender gap in anxiety?

It starts with changing the conversation. We need to stop defining girls by how they look and start valuing them for who they are. We need to teach them that their worth isn't tied to their appearance, their followers, or their ability to fit into a certain mold. And most importantly, we need to give them the tools to navigate a world that's constantly telling them they're not good enough.

Because at the end of the day, girls aren't asking for perfection—they're asking for the space to just be themselves. And that's something we can all get behind.

In the next chapter, we'll explore practical solutions for building real communities in a digital age. It's time to reconnect, both online and offline, and create spaces where everyone—regardless of gender—can thrive.

CHAPTER 6:

Social Solutions: Building Real Communities in a Digital Age

Let's face it—our world has gone digital, and there's no turning back. But here's the good news: we don't have to. It's entirely possible to live in a connected, tech-driven world while also maintaining real, meaningful connections in the physical one. In fact, it's essential for our mental health, and in 2024, we're finally seeing the first steps toward making that happen.

The solution to the anxiety epidemic isn't about unplugging from technology completely (let's be honest, no one's doing that). It's about finding balance—about reconnecting with the things that really matter: face-to-face conversations, time spent outdoors, and communities that lift us up rather than tear us down.

So, how do we start building real communities again? How do we improve mental health in an age where everything seems to revolve around screens? The answers are simpler than you might think.

The Power of In-Person Connection

Here's the first thing you need to know: humans are wired for connection. It's in our DNA. We thrive when we're part of a community, when we have people to lean on, and when we can share experiences face-to-face. In fact, studies show that **strong social connections** are one of the biggest predictors of happiness and longevity.

But over the last decade, those connections have been increasingly replaced by digital ones. Instead of calling a friend, we send a text. Instead of meeting for coffee, we like their latest Instagram post. And while those virtual interactions can be meaningful, they don't hold a candle to the power of real, in-person connection.

In 2024, researchers are doubling down on this idea. A recent study revealed that *people who spend at least two hours a week engaging in face-to-face social activities* report significantly lower levels of anxiety and depression compared to those who rely primarily on digital communication. The takeaway? Get out there and connect with people—*in real life*.

Tech-Free Zones: Schools Leading the Way

One of the most exciting developments in recent years has been the rise of **tech-free zones**, especially in schools. In 2024, more and more schools are adopting policies that limit or ban the use of smartphones during school hours, creating spaces where students can focus on learning, socializing, and just being kids—without the constant distraction of notifications.

Take **Forest Hill High School** in the UK, for example. In 2023, they introduced a *"no-phone policy"* during school hours, requiring students to lock their phones in a secure pouch at the start of the day. The result? Students reported feeling more engaged in class, more connected to their peers, and less anxious overall. One student even remarked, "It's weird, but I actually enjoy talking to people again."

These tech-free zones aren't just about eliminating distractions—they're about creating spaces where real interactions can happen. Schools are realizing that if we want to teach kids how to build strong relationships and develop emotional intelligence, we need to give them opportunities to practice those skills in the real world—not just through a screen.

Reclaiming Public Spaces for Community

Schools aren't the only places leading the charge. Across the globe, cities are reclaiming public spaces to encourage face-to-face interaction and build a sense of community. In 2024, we're seeing more *"digital detox" parks*, where Wi-Fi is deliberately not available, and benches are designed to face each other to encourage conversation.

In **Barcelona**, for example, the city has introduced "*community squares*" in residential neighborhoods. These are tech-free zones where people can come together for social activities, exercise, or just to hang out. The goal is simple: create places where people can interact, connect, and build real relationships. And it's working. Residents report feeling more connected to their neighbors, and anxiety levels in these communities have dropped significantly.

Nature as a Cure: The Rise of Outdoor Therapy

If there's one thing we've learned over the past few years, it's that nature is one of the best antidotes to anxiety. Whether it's a walk in the park, a hike in the woods, or just spending time in the garden, being outside has a profoundly positive impact on mental health.

In 2024, *"nature therapy"* is becoming more popular than ever. Schools and workplaces alike are integrating outdoor activities into their programs, recognizing that a little fresh air and sunlight can go a long way in reducing stress and boosting mood. Research backs this up: a 2023 study found that spending just *30 minutes a day outdoors* can reduce symptoms of anxiety by up to **25%**.

One particularly innovative approach is the rise of *forest schools*, where children spend a significant portion of their day learning and playing outdoors, rain or shine. These schools emphasize exploration, curiosity, and independence, helping kids develop resilience and problem-solving skills while also reaping the mental health benefits of being in nature.

Even if you're not ready to enroll your kids in a forest school, the lesson is clear: we all need more time outside. Whether it's a weekend camping trip or just a daily walk around the block, nature has a unique ability to calm our minds and remind us of the bigger picture.

Mental Health Initiatives: Normalizing Help

In 2024, mental health is no longer a taboo topic—it's front and center. More than ever, people are talking about their struggles with anxiety, depression, and stress, and there's a growing movement to make mental health resources more accessible and less stigmatized.

From schools to workplaces to community centers, initiatives aimed at improving mental health are popping up everywhere. One of the most promising trends is the rise of mental health first aid programs, where everyday people are trained to recognize the signs of anxiety and depression and offer support to those in need.

In Australia, the Mental Health First Aid program has been a huge success, with thousands of people receiving training on how to provide initial help to someone experiencing a mental health crisis. The goal is to create a culture where asking for help is not only accepted, but encouraged. And as more countries adopt similar programs, we're seeing a shift in how mental health is treated—not as a private issue to be dealt with alone, but as a community responsibility.

Redefining Success and Slowing Down

One of the biggest sources of anxiety in today's world is the constant pressure to be "*successful.*" Whether it's getting straight A's, landing the perfect job, or having a picture-perfect life on Instagram, we're all chasing some version of success—and it's wearing us down.

But in 2024, there's a growing movement to redefine what success actually looks like. Instead of measuring ourselves by external achievements, more and more people are focusing on **well-being**, **balance**, and ***personal growth***.

In places like **Denmark** and **New Zealand**, where work-life balance is highly valued, we're seeing lower rates of anxiety and higher levels of life satisfaction. These countries have embraced the idea that slowing down, taking breaks, and spending time with loved ones is just as important—if not more—than chasing the next promotion or milestone.

It's a simple idea, but one that's gaining traction: true success isn't about doing more—it's about being present, connected, and content with what you have.

What You Can Do: Practical Steps to Reconnect

So, where does that leave you? How can you start building real connections and improving your mental health in a digital world? Here are a few practical steps you can take today:

1. ***Create Tech-Free Zones***: Whether it's your dining room, your bedroom, or your entire home, designate spaces where phones, tablets, and laptops are off-limits. This will give you and your family the chance to reconnect without distractions.

2. ***Schedule Face-to-Face Time***: Make a point to meet up with friends, family, or coworkers in person. Whether it's a coffee date or a walk in the park, these interactions are key to building and maintaining strong relationships.

3. ***Get Outside***: Commit to spending at least 30 minutes a day outdoors. Whether you're walking the dog, tending to your garden, or just sitting on your porch, nature has a way of calming the mind and boosting mood.

4. ***Join a Local Group or Club***: Whether it's a book club, a hiking group, or a community service organization, joining a local group can help you meet new people and build a sense of community.

5. ***Practice Mindfulness***: Take time each day to slow down, breathe, and focus on the present moment. Mindfulness practices like meditation or journaling can help reduce anxiety and increase emotional resilience.

Building real communities in a digital age is possible—it just takes intention. By creating spaces for in-person connection, spending more time in nature, and focusing on well-being over productivity, we can begin to reclaim the parts of life that truly matter.

In the final chapter, we'll explore what governments, schools, and individuals can do to ensure that this vision becomes a reality for everyone.

CHAPTER 7:

What Parents, Teachers, and Governments Can Do (Without Panicking)

Okay, take a deep breath. If you've made it this far, you might be feeling a little overwhelmed. Yes, the digital age has brought challenges that we're only beginning to understand, and yes, it's easy to feel like we're all just one swipe away from a meltdown. But here's the good news: there's hope. And the even better news? We don't have to throw our phones in the ocean to find it.

Parents, teachers, and governments all play a crucial role in shaping how we navigate this new landscape. But let's be clear: this isn't about banning technology or creating some dystopian "no screens allowed" future. It's about finding balance, using technology mindfully, and building a world where young people can thrive—both online and offline.

So, what can we do? Let's dive into some practical, realistic solutions that don't involve panicking or setting fire to the nearest iPad.

For Parents: Lead by Example (Without the Guilt Trip)

Let's start with the parents, because, well, this is where the cycle often begins. One of the best things parents can do to help their children navigate the digital world is to model healthy behavior themselves. Now, before you start feeling guilty about all the times you've checked Instagram during dinner, relax. This isn't about being perfect—it's about being intentional.

1. Set Boundaries for Everyone (Including Yourself)
Create tech-free times and spaces in your home. Dinner time? No phones. Family game night? Screens off. It's about showing your kids that not every moment needs to be accompanied by a glowing rectangle. Research in 2024 shows that **children are more likely to adopt healthy screen habits** when they see their parents doing the same. So, if you want your kids to spend less time scrolling, lead by example.

2. Have Open Conversations
The key to helping kids manage technology isn't about policing their every move—it's about talking openly about it. Ask them how they feel after spending time on social media. Do they feel better or worse? Engaged or drained? Studies show that kids who regularly talk to their parents about their online experiences are *less likely to develop anxiety* related to social media.

3. Teach Digital Literacy
This is a big one. In 2024, digital literacy is just as important as traditional literacy. Kids need to learn how to critically evaluate what they see online, understand the motivations behind the content, and recognize when it's time to log off. As a parent, you can help by guiding them through these concepts and encouraging them to think critically about their digital lives.

For Teachers: Create Tech-Free Zones and Mindfulness in Schools

Teachers, you're on the front lines. You see the effects of digital overload every day, and you're uniquely positioned to help students strike a balance between their online and offline lives. The good news? Schools around the world are already making strides toward creating healthier, more balanced environments.

1. Implement Tech-Free Zones

In 2024, many schools are experimenting with tech-free zones, where students are encouraged (or required) to put their phones away and focus on real-world interactions. Whether it's during lunch breaks, recess, or even specific class times, these zones are designed to give students a break from the constant barrage of notifications. And guess what? It's working. Schools that have adopted these policies report that *students are more engaged* in their work, more social with their peers, and less anxious overall.

2. Encourage Mindfulness and Well-being Programs

Mindfulness isn't just for yoga retreats anymore—it's becoming a staple in classrooms around the world. In countries like Denmark and New Zealand, schools have incorporated mindfulness exercises into their daily routines to help students manage stress, focus better, and build emotional resilience. These exercises don't need to be complicated—simple breathing techniques, short meditations, or even journaling can make a big difference in reducing anxiety and helping students feel more grounded.

3. Teach Emotional Regulation

Let's be real: social media and the constant connectivity can be emotional rollercoasters. One minute you're laughing at a meme, the next you're feeling insecure because of a picture someone posted. Teaching students how to recognize and regulate their emotions in the face of these challenges is crucial. In 2024, some schools are even incorporating *emotional regulation classes* into their curriculum, giving students the tools they need to manage their feelings both online and offline.

For Governments: Policy with Purpose (Without Going Overboard)

Governments have a role to play too, and in 2024, we're seeing more and more countries step up with policies designed to protect young people from the negative effects of technology—without completely banning it.

1. Implementing Screen Time Limits for Kids
Countries like France and Japan have already passed legislation that limits screen time for children under a certain age. These policies require parents and schools to monitor how much time kids spend on devices and encourage more time spent outdoors or engaging in face-to-face activities. While these policies may seem restrictive, studies show that *limiting screen time can significantly reduce anxiety* and improve mental health in young people.

2. Regulating Social Media Platforms
In 2024, there's a growing push to hold social media platforms accountable for the impact they have on mental health. Governments are introducing regulations that require platforms like Instagram and TikTok to provide *mental health resources* directly on their apps, as well as transparency about the algorithms that prioritize certain content. Some countries are even considering laws that ban

targeted advertising to minors, which is a step toward reducing the pressure kids feel to conform to certain beauty or lifestyle standards.

3. Supporting Mental Health Initiatives

Governments can't just regulate—they also need to invest in mental health support for young people. In the UK, for example, the government has increased funding for school-based mental health counselors, making it easier for students to get help when they need it. Programs like these are essential for creating a safety net for kids who are struggling with anxiety, depression, or the effects of social media overload.

Finding Balance Without the Panic Button

At the end of the day, the key to navigating the digital world is balance. We're not living in a pre-internet age, and we don't need to pretend we are. Technology is an incredible tool—it connects us, educates us, and makes life more convenient. But like any tool, it needs to be used mindfully and with intention.

Parents, teachers, and governments all have a role to play in helping young people find that balance. And while the challenges are real, so are the solutions.

By setting boundaries, encouraging face-to-face connection, promoting digital literacy, and providing mental health support, we can create a world where technology enhances our lives without controlling them. We don't need to panic—we just need to be thoughtful about how we use the incredible tools at our disposal.

So, take a breath, close the laptop, and maybe go for a walk. The future looks a lot brighter when we remember that we're in control—not the other way around.

ABOUT THE AUTHOR

 The author is a leading expert in digital sociology and the impact of social media on modern society. With over a decade of experience researching online behaviors and their offline consequences, they bring a unique blend of academic rigor and real-world insight to the complex issues facing millennials and Gen Z in the digital age.

As a professor of Contemporary Culture and Digital Ethics at a prominent West Coast university, the author has pioneered courses on "The Psychology of Social Media" and "Digital Literacy in the 21st Century." Their research on the effects of constant connectivity on mental health has been published in several peer-reviewed journals and cited in major media outlets.

Before entering academia, the author spent several years working in Silicon Valley, gaining firsthand experience of the tech industry's inner workings. This background provides a

DR. SAMANTHA MITCHELL

nuanced understanding of both the benefits and pitfalls of our increasingly digital lives.

A frequent speaker at international conferences on technology and society, the author is known for their ability to translate complex social theories into accessible, actionable advice. Their previous works include articles on digital wellbeing, the ethics of AI, and the changing landscape of human interaction in the age of smartphones.

When not writing or teaching, the author enjoys disconnecting from technology through hiking, community gardening, and practicing mindfulness – always with their smartphone safely tucked away.

"**The Anxious Thumb**" is the culmination of years of research, personal experience, and countless conversations with individuals navigating the challenges of life in the social media era.

www.ingramcontent.com/pod-product-compliance
Lightning Source LLC
Chambersburg PA
CBHW030054230526
45471CB00003B/1099